NATALIE GRANT
RELENTLESS

Photographer: Dominick Guillemot

Shawnee Press, Inc.
1107 17th Avenue South • Nashville, TN 37212
A Subsidiary of **Music Sales Corporation**

Visit Shawnee Press Online at
www.shawneepress.com/songbooks

SB1028

NATALIE GRANT
RELENTLESS

CONTENTS

I Will Not Be Moved

Words and Music by
NATALIE GRANT

though I have been torn,

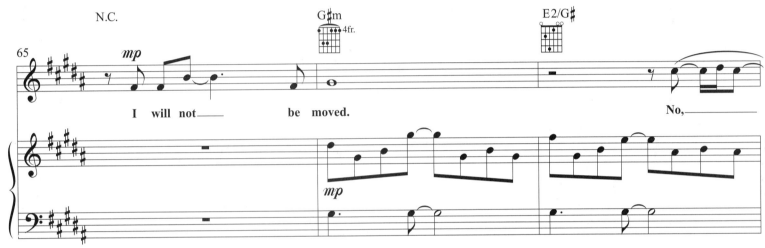

I will not be moved.   No,

no.   I will not be moved.

No,   I will not be moved.

In Better Hands

Words and Music by
JIM DADDARIO *and* **THOM HARDWELL**

free ____ if you don't reach for help, ____ and you can't____

love ____ if you don't love____ your - self. ____

There is hope when my faith ____ runs ____ out,

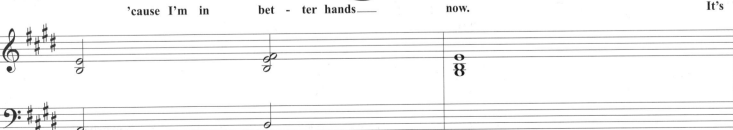

'cause I'm in bet - ter hands____ now. It's

So, take this heart of mine, there's no doubt

I'm in bet - ter hands now.

It's like the sun is shin - ing when the rain

Make It Matter

Words and Music by
NATALIE GRANT, BERNIE HERMS
and **MATTHEW WEST**

it's on-ly You I'm chas-ing af - ter. Take this life and make it mat - ter.

Help me give— more than— I take,

Back at My Heart

Words and Music by
NATALIE GRANT, BERNIE HERMS
and **MATTHEW WEST**

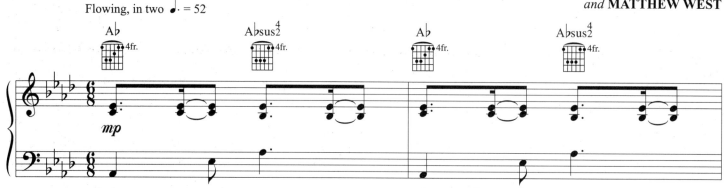

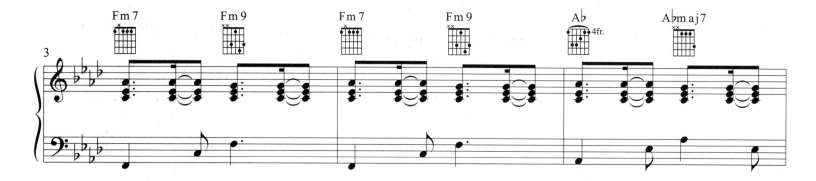

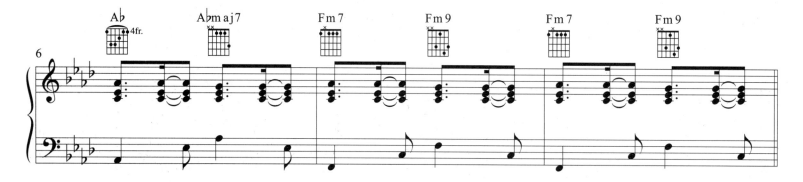

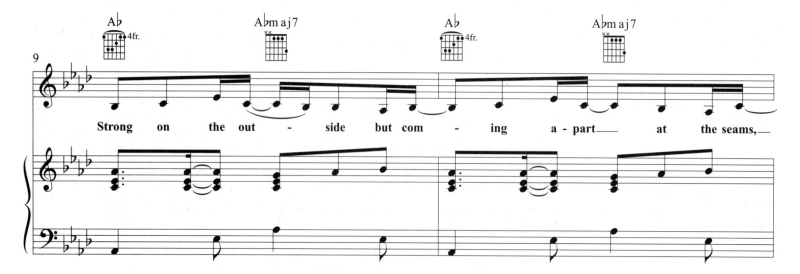

Strong on the out - side but com - ing a - part___ at the seams,___

Let Go

Words and Music by
NATALIE GRANT, BEN GLOVER
and **SHAUN SHANKEL**

CODA

Don't wan-na o - ver - think it, don't wan-na wor-ry so much. Gon-na

live my life and not lose touch. I'm gon-na let go.

Yeah,

yeah.

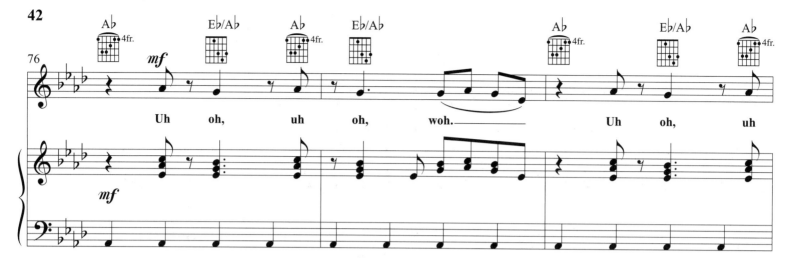

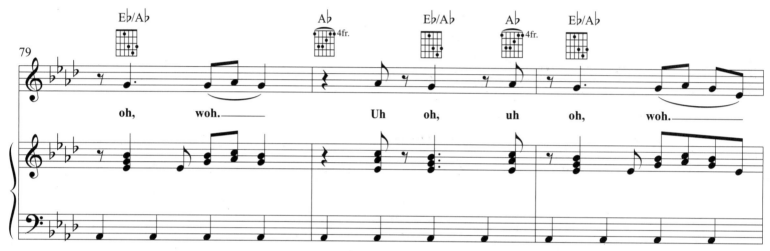

Perfect People

Words and Music by
JASON BARTON, SAM MIZELL
and **MATTHEW WEST**

Never let 'em see you when you're break-ing, and never let 'em see you when you fall. That's how we live,

and be a-mazed _____ and be changed _____ by a per-fect God. _____

_____ Yeah. _____

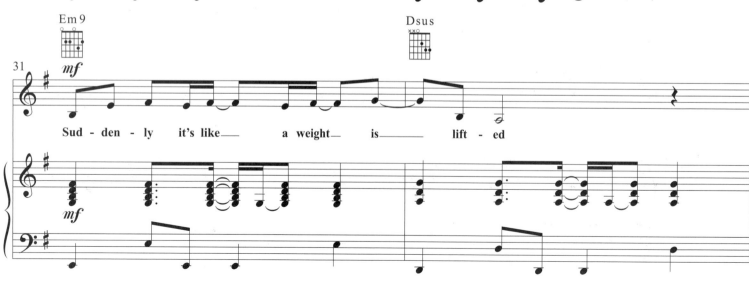

Sud - den - ly it's like _____ a weight _____ is _____ lift - ed

Our Hope Endures

Words and Music by
CHRISTA WELLS *and* **NATALIE GRANT**

you as-sume____ that this one has suf-fered her share,

life will be kind - er from here. Oh, but some-times the sun___

___ stays hid-den____ for years, some-times the sky___ rains night af-ter night.

___ When will it clear?_____ But our hope en -

So Long

Words and Music by
NATALIE GRANT

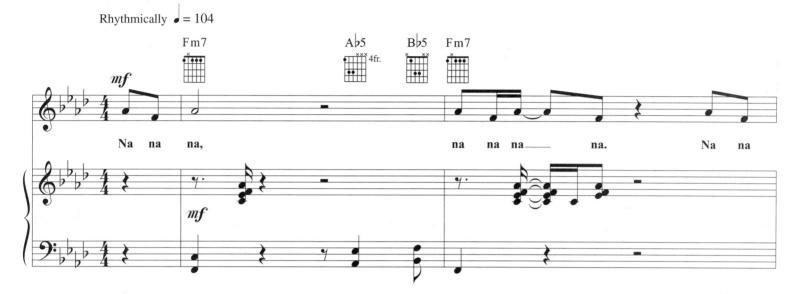

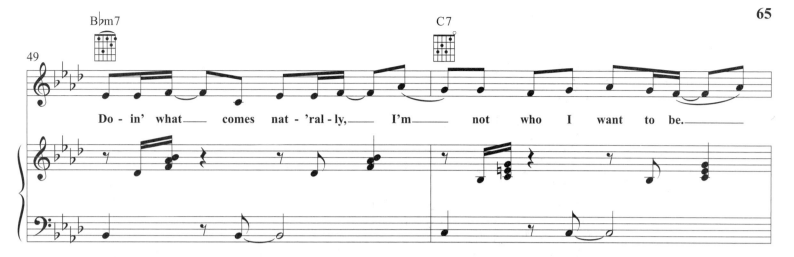

Do- in' what___ comes nat-'ral-ly,___ I'm___ not who I want to be.___

Read-y to,___ I'm read-y to___ be free, oh___ yeah.___ So long,___

D.S. al CODA 𝄋

CODA

gone, gone,___ gone.___ So long.___

___ Yeah, yeah,___ yeah, yeah, yeah, so long.___

Na na na na na na na, so long.

So long, yeah. Na na na,

C7   Fm7

na na na na. Hey, hey, hey, so long. Na na

C7

na, na na na na. Hey, hey, hey, so long,

yeah. So long, fare-well to my old

self. Good-bye to the lie that I can't be some-one else.

'Cause who I was ain't who I am. I know that I've

been born a - gain. Those stains of my his -

Wonderful Life

Words and Music by
SHAUN SHANKEL and TRINA HARMON

it slow - ly. _____ All our time _____ is fly - ing by

too fast. _____ Where we're head -

- ed is - n't al - ways clear; _____ it can feel _____ like no - where. _____

But ev - 'ry - thing _____ we need is here, right now.

-ing, and it's so___ good to be a-live._____

Cue: 2nd time only

Ev - 'ry - thing's___ all right,_____ 'cause all___

___ we've ev - er need-ed___ is a per-fect___ day___ to be___ a-live.

So no___ more wait - ing now.___ ___ more wait-ing now___

for a won - der - ful life, _____ 'cause it's a won - der - ful

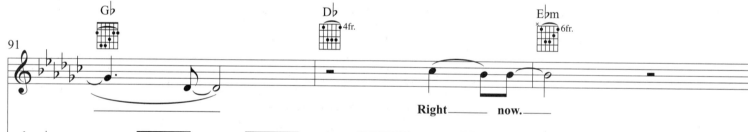

life _____ right now. _____ Oh, yeah. ____

Right _____ now. _____

Oh. _____

Safe

Words and Music by
SHAUN SHANKEL, TYLER HAYES-BIECK
and **TIFFANY LEE**

Lyrics:

How did You know____ that I'm all a-lone____ to-day?____

Oh, I feel so scared,____ and I want to go____

Make a Way

Words and Music by
NATALIE GRANT

Slowly, with much emotion ♩ = 72

She was on - ly sev - en-teen, wild at heart___ and fol - low-ing___ her

bi - tion would be her drive._____ She cried: I'll make a way,_____

hope that kept___ her dreams a - live._____

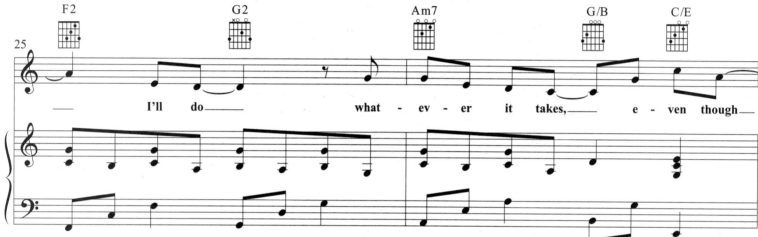

— I'll do_____ what - ev - er it takes,_____ e - ven though___

— it won't___ be eas - y._____ I have a plan,___

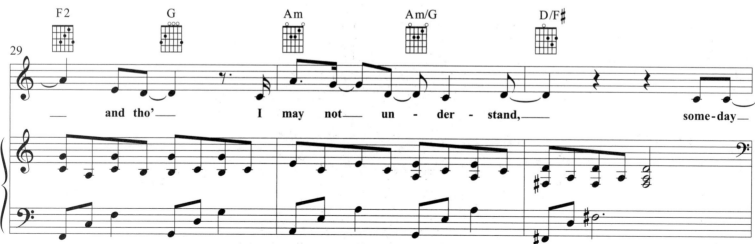

— and tho'___ I may not___ un - der - stand,_____ some-day___

out there may-be there was some-thing more. And so she bowed

her head to pray. And she cried,

"Je-sus, please make a way." And she

heard Him say: I'll make a way, I'll do what-

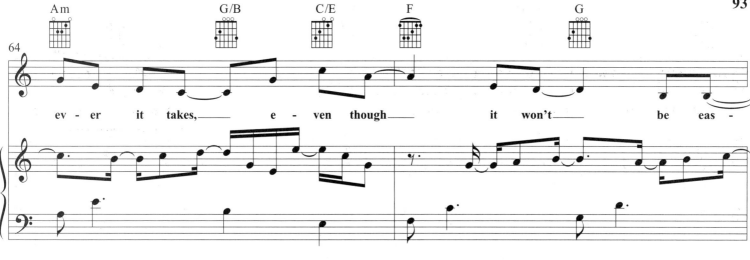

ev - er it takes,_____ e - ven though_____ it won't_____ be eas -

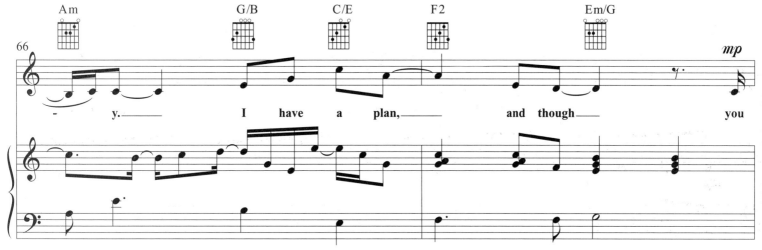

- y._____ I have a plan,_____ and though_____ you

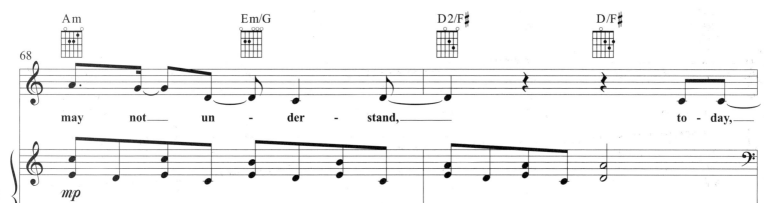

may not_____ un - der - stand,_____ to - day,_____

_____ I'll make_____ a way._____ Hear Him say: To - day_____

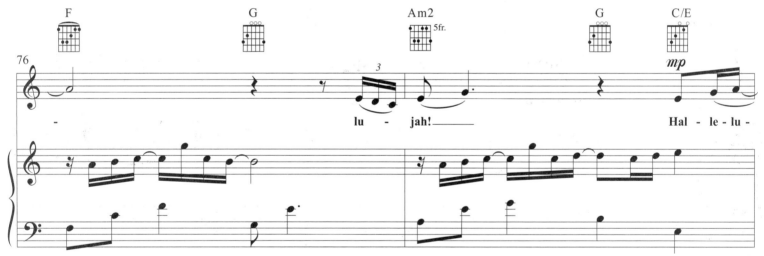

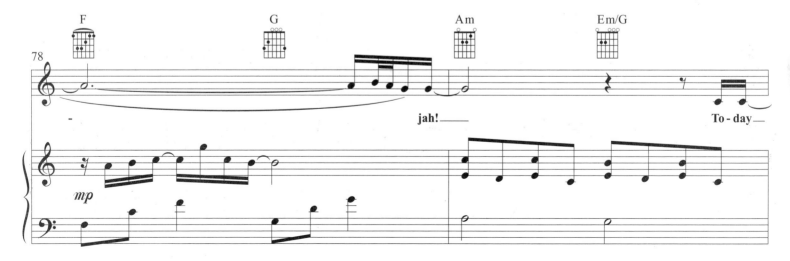

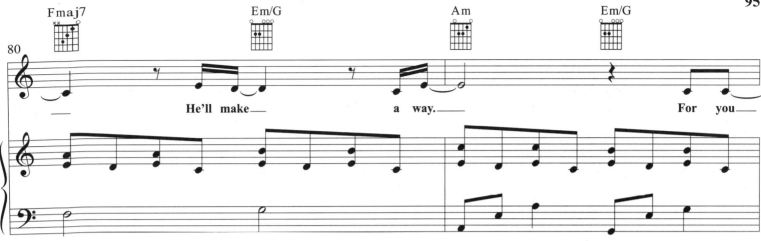

He'll make— a way.— For you—

He's gon-na make a way.— For you—

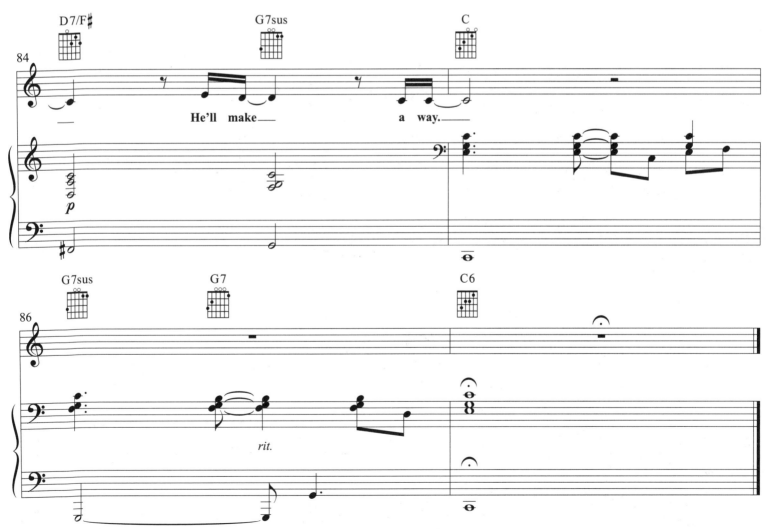

He'll make— a way.—

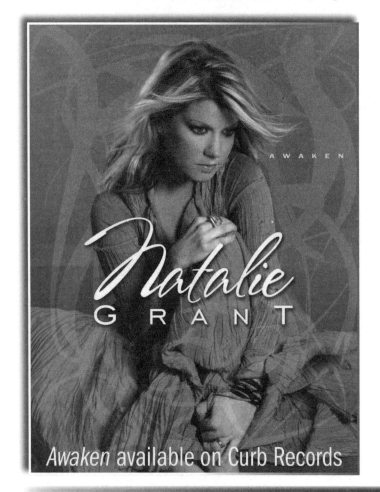